What Does a Screwdriver Do?

by Robin Nelson

first step nonfiction

Lerner Publications Company · Minneapolis

What tool is this?

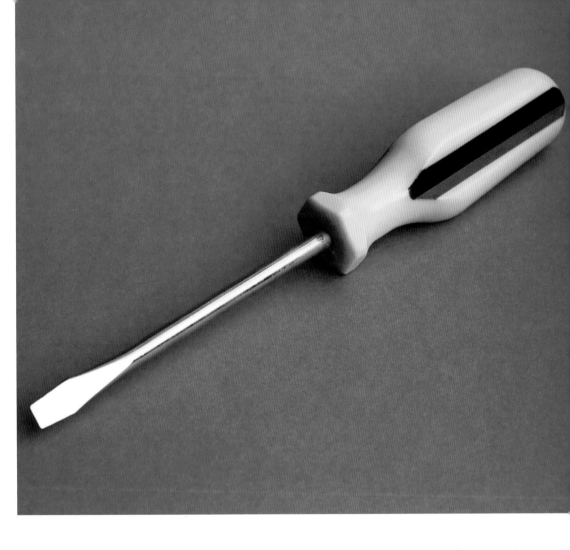

It is a screwdriver.

Tools help us do jobs.

Screwdrivers make jobs easier.

There are many different
kinds of screwdrivers. They
6 come in many sizes.

These are **screws**. The tip
of the screwdriver must fit
into the top of the screw.

This screwdriver has a flat tip.

It is used for screws with
one **slot** on top.

This screwdriver has a pointed tip.

It is used for screws with an *X* on top.

This is the handle of the screwdriver.

We hold the handle. We
fit the tip into the screw
and turn.

People use screwdrivers to tighten light switches.

People use screwdrivers to open things.

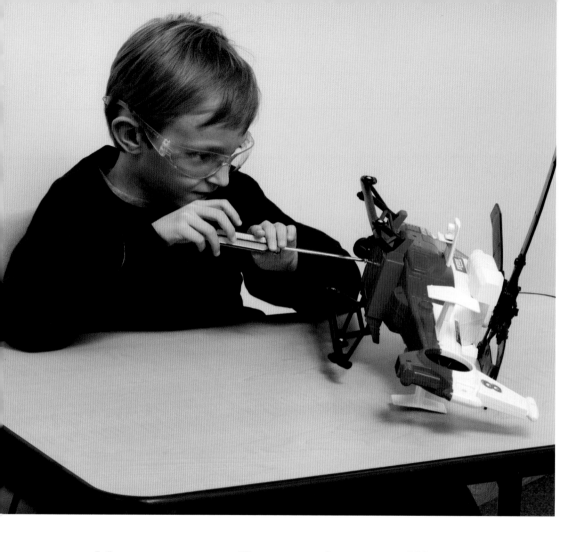

You can fix a toy with a screwdriver.

What else can you do with a screwdriver?

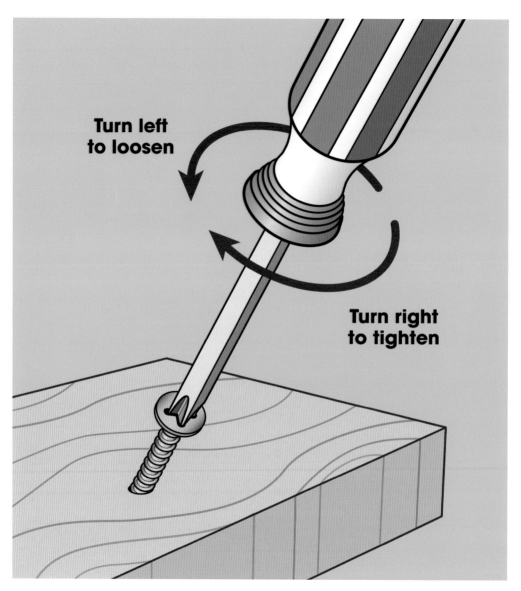

Turn left to loosen

Turn right to tighten

How Screws Work

Screws are simple machines. A screw is a **rod** with a **thread** around it. When you turn a screwdriver, you make the screw turn too. Each turn pushes the screw deeper into the wood. The thread pulls on the wood and holds the screw in place.

Safety First

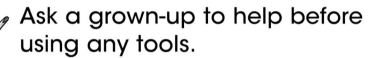 Ask a grown-up to help before using any tools.

Wear safety glasses to protect your eyes.

Roll up your sleeves. Tuck in your shirt. Tie back your hair. Remove any jewelry that might get in the way.

 Carry a screwdriver with the point down and away from your body.

Never run with a tool in your hand.

Be careful not to poke your fingers.

Put away the screwdriver and screws when you are done with your job.

Glossary

 rod – a straight, thin bar

 screw – a metal rod that has a top and a thread that wraps around it

 slot – a small, narrow cut in the surface of something

 thread – a thin, bumpy line

Index

The images in this book are used with the permission of: © Timages/Dreamstime.com, pp. 2, 3; © Franz Pfuegl/Dreamstime.com, p. 4; © Zave Smith/Uppercut Images/Getty Images, p. 5; © Stockbyte/Getty Images, p. 6 (top); © iStockphoto.com/Ni Qin, p. 6 (bottom); © Todd Strand/ Independent Picture Service, pp. 7, 9, 12, 16, 17, 22 (second from top) (third from top); © Brand X Pictures/Getty Images, p. 8; © iStockphoto.com/Mark Herreid, p. 10; © Rubberball/Mike Kemp/Getty Images, p. 11; © Dorling Kindersley/The Agency Collection/Getty Images, p. 13; © Medioimages/Photodisc/Getty Images, p. 14; © John A. Rizzo/Photodisc/Getty Images, p. 15; © Laura Westlund/Independent Picture Service, pp. 18, 20-21, 22 (top) (bottom).

Front cover: © Yari/Dreamstime.com.

Main body text set in ITC Avant Garde Gothic Std Medium 21/25.
Typeface provided by Adobe Systems.

Lerner Publications Company
A division of Lerner Publishing Group, Inc.
241 First Avenue North
Minneapolis, MN 55401 U.S.A.

Website address: www.lernerbooks.com

Library of Congress Cataloging-in-Publication Data

Nelson, Robin, 1971–
      What does a screwdriver do? / by Robin Nelson.
         p.   cm. — (First step nonfiction–tools at work)
      Includes index.
      ISBN 978–0–7613–8978–1 (lib. bdg. : alk. paper)
      1. Screwdrivers—Juvenile literature. I. Title.
   TJ1201.S34N45 2013
   621.9'72—dc23   2011039077

Manufactured in the United States of America
1 – CG – 7/15/12